GEORGE WASHINGTON CARVER

Essential Lives

GEORGE WASHINGTON CARVER

AGRICULTURAL INNOVATOR

by **Helga Schier**

Content Consultant:
Gary R. Kremer, Executive Director
The State Historical Society of Missouri

ABDO
Publishing Company

CREDITS

Published by ABDO Publishing Company, 8000 West 78th Street, Edina, Minnesota 55439. Copyright © 2008 by Abdo Consulting Group, Inc. International copyrights reserved in all countries. No part of this book may be reproduced in any form without written permission from the publisher. The Essential Library™ is a trademark and logo of ABDO Publishing Company.

Printed in the United States.

Editor: Rebecca Rowell
Copy Editor: Paula Lewis
Interior Design and Production: Rebecca Daum
Cover Design: Rebecca Daum

Library of Congress Cataloging-in-Publication Data
Schier, Helga.
  George Washington Carver / Helga Schier.
      p. cm.— (Essential lives)
  Includes bibliographical references.
  ISBN 978-1-60453-035-3
  1. Carver, George Washington, 1864?-1943—Juvenile literature.
2. African American agriculturists—Biography—Juvenile
literature. 3. Agriculturists—United States—Biography—Juvenile
literature. I. Title.

S417.C3S35 2008
630.92—dc22
[B]
                                    2007030841

TABLE OF CONTENTS

Chapter 1

George Washington Carver was an agriculture expert.

A DAZZLING PERFORMANCE

On January 21, 1921, a middle-aged man in a worn suit spoke before the Ways and Means Committee of the U.S. House of Representatives. George Washington Carver had come to Washington, D.C., on behalf of the United Peanut Association of America in support of a proposed tax on imported peanuts. He was given ten minutes to argue his point—just ten minutes to convince the men on the committee that U.S. peanut farmers needed protection against competition from other countries.

The United States had been importing large amounts of peanuts for some time. Carter believed the imported peanuts were inferior to those grown in the United States. In addition, he had discovered and promoted many uses for the peanut, including foods, cosmetics, household products, and natural fertilizer. Carver had also worked to help African-American farmers in the South become better farmers. His success before the committee would assist peanut farmers, particularly those he devoted so much time and energy to helping. Given the

House Ways and Means Committee

The Committee on Ways and Means of the U.S. House of Representatives handles some of the most important financial matters of the U.S. government. This includes:
- Taxation
- International tariffs
- Social Security
- Unemployment benefits
- Medicare and Medicaid
- Welfare

The U.S. Constitution requires that all bills regarding taxation must originate in the House of Representatives. As part of the process in the House, taxation bills go through the Ways and Means Committee. The committee is considered the most powerful committee of the House. Its members are not allowed to serve on any other committees.

George Washington Carver's presentation to the Ways and Means Committee in 1921 resulted in a tariff on foreign peanuts that saved U.S. peanut farmers.

importance of the tariff to the many farmers who grew peanuts, ten minutes was little time for Carver to make his case.

A veteran speaker and teacher, Carver was not intimidated by having limited time to make his point. He slowly unpacked the box he had brought, spending much of his ten minutes placing several containers on the table. He had brought different products made from peanuts, including peanut milk, instant coffee, flour, and cheese. Carver also brought a breakfast cereal. As he put the cereal on the table he said, "I am very sorry you cannot taste this so I will taste it for you."[1] While most of the committee members were entertained by and receptive to Carver, Connecticut Representative John Q. Tilson responded to Carver's statement with a racial remark. Carver replied coolly and continued with his talk. Tilson made no further remarks during the remainder of Carver's presentation.

Carver showed more and more samples of peanut products. When Carver expressed his belief that foreign peanuts were not as good as those grown in the United States, Illinois Representative Henry T. Rainey debated Carver. Rainey commented that "we need not fear these inferior peanuts from abroad." Carver replied, "Sometimes you have to protect a good thing." After further debate, Carver had the final word, saying, "That is all the tariff means—to put the other fellow out of business."[2] The exchange was well received by committee members, who laughed during the debate. By the time Carver's ten

Highlights of 1921

Prohibition was in full force. Organized crime existed. It was the time of the silent film. Popular actors of the day included Buster Keaton and Greta Garbo. Albert Einstein was awarded the Nobel Prize in Physics.

minutes were up, the politicians were hooked by his presentation.

The committee allowed Carver unlimited time to argue his case. He showed that the peanut was not an inferior crop and the potential market for peanut products was well worth protection from foreign imports. Carver spoke for almost an hour before the House Ways and Means Committee. His presentation was a success. As a result of his talk with the committee, the U.S. government imposed a tariff on imported peanuts the following year. The American peanut farmers were safe from foreign competitors. One spokesman of the peanut industry said of Carver's presentation, "He not only pleased the committee, but convinced them in no uncertain way that the peanut industry was worth protecting and preserving for American farmers."[3]

On that January day in 1921, George Washington Carver dazzled the men of the Ways and Means Committee and the onlookers in attendance. The people even applauded when Carver finished his speech. He impressed them with his knowledge of agriculture—particularly peanut farming—and with his performance. Carver's success with the committee was quite an accomplishment at the time. He was an African-American man during a time when segregation was a way of life in the South. At a time when African Americans were often looked down upon by whites, Carver was a well-respected agricultural expert.

Carver's work would lead to even greater successes than swaying the federal government to help U.S. peanut farmers. Carver impressed more than the politicians with

No Formal Education for African Americans

When African Americans were enslaved in the United States, they were denied a formal education. Most Southern states had made it illegal to teach slaves how to read and write. Even after the Civil War, it was difficult for African Americans to receive a good formal education or vocational training. Segregation laws divided African-American and white students, often placing them in separate schools. Segregated public services were supposed to be separate but equal—they were anything but equal. African-American schools often were vastly inferior to white schools. Schools were often in poor shape—some with only one bathroom for all the students and teachers to share—or overcrowded, and class offerings were often limited compared to those of white schools.

With limited training and education, African Americans struggled to become professionals in occupations other than those typically performed as slaves: domestic servants, manual laborers, or field workers. Despite fewer educational opportunities, some African Americans obtained educational and vocational training by overcoming tremendous opposition and hardship. Many later went on to make significant contributions to American life and science.

his knowledge and presence. His witty testimony before the Ways and Means Committee was widely reported and built the foundation for his fame as a scientist and educator. As a scientist, Carver's goal was to improve and expand the market possibilities of southern crops such as the peanut and the sweet potato. As an educator, Carver strived to aid African-American farmers, most of them impoverished and illiterate, by teaching them how to farm more efficiently. His work with the farmers helped revitalize the economy in the region.

Peanut Butter Today

Peanut butter might be in need of another hearing before a federal committee. The popular sandwich spread has come under attack because of studies on food allergies and the fact that some Americans are allergic to nuts. Although only 1.5 to 2 percent of Americans suffer from peanut allergies, many school districts across the United States have banned peanut butter.

Carver was hailed as the savior of southern agriculture. He was a folk hero. More than that, he rose to international fame from the humblest of beginnings, becoming one African-American man whose life and work would find their place in the hearts of people of all ages, races, and backgrounds. George Washington Carver became a shining example of the successes that can be achieved with hard work, determination, and faith.

George Washington Carver

This statue at the George Washington Carver National Monument represents Carver's love of nature as a child.

A THIRST FOR KNOWLEDGE

George Washington Carver was born on a farm near Diamond Grove, Missouri, in 1864 or 1865. The exact date of his birth is unknown. The identity of his father is also unknown. George and his older brother, Jim, were born to

Mary, a slave on the farm of Moses Carver. An Ohio-born homesteader, Carver did not condone slavery but had purchased Mary to get much-needed help for his prospering farm.

Though Missouri was a slave state, it never seceded, or separated, from the Union during the Civil War. As a result, tensions in the state were extremely high between those who supported the North and those who supported the South. Toward the end of the Civil War, when George was born, ambushes, murder, and farm raids between Unionist "jayhawkers" and Confederate "bushwhackers" were common.

For reasons that are unknown, Moses Carver was a target of bushwhackers. During one raid on his farm, Mary and infant George were abducted. Carver was determined to get them back. He asked a neighbor, a Union scout who knew the Confederate bushwhacker hideouts well, to go after them. A few days later, the neighbor returned with George, but only after Carver paid the kidnappers with a prized horse. Mary was never found. Carver and his wife, Susan, raised George and Jim as though the boys were their own children.

LIFE ON A FARM

George grew up much like the other children in the area. Being raised on a farm meant hard work. Jim helped Moses Carver maintain the farm. George, who was somewhat frail and often suffered from respiratory problems, helped Susan Carver in the house.

George had a tremendous curiosity. He spent his spare time in the woods examining plant and animal life. He quickly developed a particular talent for growing plants. He even became known as the plant doctor in the area. Many local residents would bring their ailing flowers

The Civil War

The American Civil War between 1861 and 1865 divided the United States. Led by President Abraham Lincoln, the United States was opposed by 11 Southern states that seceded, or separated, from the Union and formed the Confederate States of America. These states elected their own president, Jefferson Davis.

The issue of slavery was at the root of economic, moral, and political differences between the North and the South. The agricultural South feared that the industrial North, which grew much faster, would soon control the entire Union and no longer represent the interests of the South. Southern states insisted that, in an effort to protect their individual states' interests, they had a right to secede. Southern Confederates attacked the Union military installation in Fort Sumter, at Charleston, South Carolina, in April 1861. President Lincoln sent troops to protect the fort. The Civil War had begun. The war resulted in almost 1 million soldiers and citizens dead or wounded and unparalleled destruction and devastation, particularly in the South.

to him. Even though Moses and Susan Carver recognized George's intelligence and supported his talents, there was little opportunity for formal education or training.

LEAVING HOME

Moses and Susan Carver supported George's desire to learn and encouraged his pursuit of a formal education. In 1877, Moses Carver allowed George to go away to a school for African Americans in Neosho, Missouri. George had to walk the 11 miles (18 km) from his home to Neosho. When he arrived at school, George had little food left and no lodging for the night. Legend has it that he simply took shelter in a barn and was awakened the next day by its owners, Andrew and Mariah Watkins. In exchange for helping with household chores, the childless couple took him in.

Within a year of going to Neosho, George had learned all he could there. In 1878, with the support of both the Carvers and the Watkinses, George moved to Fort Scott, Kansas. There, he worked doing whatever job he could find, going to school when he could. He was completely on his own. He was poor and hungry, but he was learning.

On March 26, 1879, George witnessed a brutal lynching of an African-American man accused of attacking a 12-year-old white girl. Although more typical for the South, lynching was frequent across the country at the time. Terrified by what he had seen, George left Fort Scott.

After Fort Scott, George lived with the Seymours, an African-American family, in Olathe, Kansas. He then moved to Minneapolis, Kansas. Using his domestic skills, George opened a laundry to make enough money to support himself and to attend school. While in school, George nurtured his botanical talent. He also began to paint and play music. George completed high school in Minneapolis in 1885 and planned to go to college.

WHITES ONLY

George applied to Highland College in Highland, Kansas, and was accepted. However, he was turned away when he arrived at the school's gates. Highland College was an all-white school.

Because he had applied by mail, school officials had not realized George was African-American. The school's message was clear: higher education was for whites only. Frustrated, he gave up the idea of going to college. Following in Moses Carver's footsteps, George pursued homesteading. He farmed 17 acres (7 ha) of land in Ness County, Kansas. He participated in the life of the community, joining the literary society and playing music at local dances. While he later expressed his appreciation of this period in Ness County, the fierce weather made life hard. Homesteading was not for him. In 1889, George left Ness County to seek his luck elsewhere. In 1890, he arrived in Winterset, Iowa, where he was hired as a hotel cook. He also opened a laundry. While in Winterset, George met the Milhollands, a white couple. The couple befriended George and encouraged him to attend Simpson College, a small liberal arts college run by Methodists in nearby Indianola, Iowa. George applied, this time making sure that the color of his skin was made clear from the start. He was accepted.

Carver's Special Abilities

The citizens of Ness County, Kansas, saw first-hand Carver's abilities. One white man remarked, "When I was in the presence of that young man Carver, as a white man, of the supposed dominant race, I was humiliated by my own inadequacy of knowledge, compared to his."[1]

This oil painting by Carver reflects his love of nature.

COLLEGE LIFE

George was the only African American on Simpson's campus. He was also poorer than any other student. Still, the faculty and his fellow students did their best to make George feel as welcome as any other student. He supported himself doing other students' laundry. He enrolled in art classes and developed considerable skills as a painter. Etta Budd, his art teacher, was the daughter of a horticulture professor at Iowa State College. Though she was impressed with George's artistic skills, Budd believed he could not get a job as an artist, so she encouraged him to transfer to Iowa State College to pursue a degree in science.

In 1891, after a year at Simpson College, George moved to Ames, Iowa, and enrolled at Iowa State College of Agricultural and Mechanical Arts. His time there was difficult at first. Once again, he was the only African American on campus. This time, though, George did not feel as welcomed as he had at Simpson. Instead, other students called him derogatory names during his first day on campus, his lodging was inadequate, and he was not allowed to eat with the other students in the dining hall. But the situation soon became positive for George.

A Talented Painter

Although George Washington Carver never became a professional painter, his talent as a painter was acknowledged and celebrated in many exhibits during his lifetime. The first, and perhaps most significant, exhibit was during the 1893 World's Fair in Chicago, Illinois.

As always, George held tight to his faith and religious beliefs during the challenging first days at Iowa State College. This proved helpful in breaking down barriers and connecting him with others on campus. He and some fellow students began holding prayer meetings. The meetings led George to James A. Wilson, a faculty member. Director of the Iowa Agricultural Experiment Station, Wilson was, similar to George, a devout Christian. The two men formed a strong bond as a result of the prayer meetings and their shared beliefs. This relationship and the extracurricular activities George participated in helped ease his transition to the school.

George was an exceptional student, particularly in botany and horticulture. His teachers soon recognized his considerable skill in grafting and cross-fertilizing plants. These methods of modifying plants can create new plants that are more resilient and useful than their natural originals. George's skills were remarkable. When Carver completed his bachelor of agriculture degree in 1894, his teachers urged him to stay on to pursue a master's degree. George stayed and was assigned to a faculty member, L.H. Pammel, to do research. Pammel was an expert at mycology, the study of fungi. As

Pammel mentored graduate student Carver at Iowa State College.

a mentor, Pammel instilled what would become
Carver's lifelong interest in the research of fungi
and plant diseases. In his postgraduate research with
Pammel, George discovered a particular fungus that
had caused problems for the soybean for decades
and offered suggestions for treating the plant
successfully. Pammel referred to Carver's talent as

a researcher by calling him "the best collector I ever had in the department or have ever known."[2]

Carver proved to be such a gifted graduate student, researcher, and teacher that his future as a faculty member at Iowa Sate College seemed assured. As completion of his graduate degree neared, George had several employment options, including an offer from Alcorn Agricultural and Mechanical College, an African-American school in Mississippi. George's teachers expressed their interest in wanting him to stay at Iowa State College. James Wilson wrote of George:

> *In cross-fertilization … and the propagation of plants, Carver is by all means the ablest student we have here. Except for the respect I owe the professors, I would say he is fully abreast of them and exceeds in special lines in which he has a taste.*

> *We have nobody to take his place and I would never part with a student with so much regret as George Carver. … I think he feels at home among us, but you call for him to go down there and teach agriculture and horticulture … to the people of his own race, a people I have been taught to respect, and for whose religious education we consider it a privilege to contribute. I cannot object to his going. … It will be difficult, in fact impossible to fill his place.[3]*

A JOB OFFER

George had developed a strong sense of responsibility toward African-American people and felt that it was his duty to help improve their quality of life. In March 1896, George received an offer to join the faculty of the Tuskegee Normal and Industrial Institute (Tuskegee Institute), an African-American college in Tuskegee, Alabama. As the only African American in the country who had graduate-level training, he was the natural choice to become the head of the school's new Department of Agriculture.

The position would not provide a better salary or better research facilities than Iowa State College. To the contrary, it would require hard work under financially strained circumstances. But it would also give George an opportunity to teach African Americans and to provide some of them with an education.

**A Job Offer
from Tuskegee**

In the spring of 1896, Booker T. Washington wrote to Carver, asking him to join the staff of Tuskegee Institute:

"Tuskegee Institute seeks to provide education—a means for survival to those who attend. Our students are poor, often starving. They travel miles of torn roads, across years of poverty now. We teach them to read and write, but words cannot fill stomachs. They need to learn how to plant and harvest crops. …

I cannot offer you money, position or fame. The first two you have. The last, from the place you occupy, you will no doubt achieve.

These things I now ask you to give up. I offer you in their place—work—hard, hard work—the challenge of bringing people from degradation, poverty and waste to full manhood."[4]

George accepted the job offer. In the fall of 1896, equipped with his newly awarded master's degree, George moved to Alabama. ⌐

"Of course it has always been the one great ideal of my life to be of the greatest good to the greatest number of 'my people' possible and to this end I have been preparing my self [sic] for these many years; feeling as I do that this line of education is the key to unlock the golden door of freedom to our people."[5]
—*George Washington Carver in a letter to Booker T. Washington, April 12, 1896*

George Washington Carver's graduation photo at Iowa State College (now Iowa State University), 1894

Carver studied plants and agriculture, sharing his extensive knowledge with students and farmers.

A Formidable Teacher

George Washington Carver had undoubtedly experienced discrimination in his lifetime. Alabama and the South, however, provided new levels of discrimination. Aid provided to African Americans by the federal government during the South's period of Reconstruction (1865–1877) was inadequate and short-lived. Even though the war brought freedom from slavery, it did not bring freedom from poverty and hardship. It also did not bring equality. While no longer slaves, African Americans were still considered and treated as second-class citizens.

Ratification of the Fifteenth Amendment in 1870 granted African Americans the right to vote. However, the amendment applied to adult African-American males. Even with the Fifteenth Amendment, they often had difficulty voting because of local laws that applied in certain situations. For example, some Southern states imposed laws that required African-American voters to pay poll taxes or pass literacy tests in order to vote. These rules excluded the mostly poor and illiterate African-American men from voting. Known as Jim Crow laws, these laws were passed in the late 1800s and early 1900s to keep African Americans separate from and subordinate to whites.

SEPARATE BUT UNEQUAL

The 1896 U.S. Supreme Court decision of *Plessy v. Ferguson* set forth the policy "separate but equal" that confirmed and validated the legal practice of segregation. However, segregated facilities were far from equal. Political, social, or economic equality seemed out of reach for many African Americans, especially in the South.

Prejudice and stereotyping made social integration all but impossible, branding African Americans as inferior. They were accused of many crimes. The South became a dangerous place for African Americans.

Economic inequality was also an issue in the South. Most African Americans in the South were sharecroppers on

Jim Crow Laws

Beginning in the late 1800s, laws were passed by Southern states that attempted to keep African Americans and whites socially separate. These laws affected all areas of life: education, health care, housing, marriage, work, transportation, and socializing. A sample of these laws included:

- Florida: "The schools for white children and the schools for negro children shall be conducted separately."
- Virginia: "Any public hall, theatre, opera house, motion picture show, or place of public entertainment which is attended by both white and colored persons shall separate the white race and the colored race."
- Alabama: "No person or corporation shall require any white female nurse to nurse in wards or rooms in hospitals, either public or private, in which negro men are placed."
- Louisiana: "Any person ... who shall rent any part of any such building to a negro person or a negro family when such building is already in whole or in part in occupancy by a white person or white family shall be guilty of a misdemeanor."[1]

land owned by a handful of wealthy whites. In exchange for farming the land, sharecroppers were entitled to a share of the proceeds from the sale of their crops. Sharecropping prompted farmers to plant the crop that promised the fastest and biggest return so that their share of the proceeds—often less than half—would buy enough food to survive. Because they lived in such dire conditions and did not own the land, sharecroppers disregarded the long-term effects of their farming on the land. Their hard work was done with poor agricultural methods and with little return.

This is why Tuskegee Institute hired Carver. The school hoped that Carver would provide some of the agricultural training the farmers so desperately needed.

BOOKER T. WASHINGTON

Tuskegee Institute was headed by Booker T. Washington, a premier African-American leader of

Separate but Equal

The 1896 Supreme Court decision in *Plessy v. Ferguson* claimed a constitutional right of the individual states to create different public facilities for African Americans and whites. This legalized the practice of segregation. The decision argued that as long as the facilities—public transportation, restaurants, and schools—were the same in quality, separate facilities did not classify African Americans as inferior and, therefore, did not violate the civil rights of former slaves as guaranteed by the Thirteenth and Fourteenth Amendments, which had been added to the U.S. Constitution after the Civil War.

Booker T. Washington

the time. Washington thought political and social
equality for African Americans would evolve from
economic independence. He firmly believed that
self-improvement, particularly economic self-
improvement, would lead to a better future for
African Americans. Tuskegee Institute was built and
developed to teach African Americans the practical
skills that would make them employable by the
white elite. On September 18, 1895, Washington

spoke to a predominantly white audience at the Cotton States and International Exposition in Atlanta, Georgia. In his speech, later known as "The Atlanta Compromise," Washington promoted African Americans as willing participants in the reconstruction of the South. He urged whites to employ African Americans rather than new immigrants from Europe—African Americans had already proven their value to whites by tending plantations during slavery "without strikes and labor wars."[2] In his speech, Washington advocated peaceful coexistence of the races, a skillful accommodation to the reality of segregation.

Carver was a living example of what Washington advocated. Despite adversity, Carver's diligence and hard work had earned him a graduate degree from a respected white university in a marketable discipline.

Booker T. Washington

Booker Taliaferro Washington was born on a tobacco farm in Virginia on April 5, 1856. His mother, an African American, was a cook. His father, who was white, was from a nearby farm. After the Thirteenth Amendment formally freed slaves in 1865, his family moved to West Virginia.

At 16, Washington returned to Virginia to attend Hampton Institute, a new school for African Americans. He eventually became an instructor there. In 1881, he founded Tuskegee Institute and served as its principal.

Considered the top African-American educator at the time, Washington was criticized because he did not fight segregation. He accommodated rather than challenged segregation. This was partly because he needed support from whites who were in power. However, Washington's policy of accommodation changed later in his life.

Washington died on November 15, 1915. He was 59 years old.

"To those of the white race who look to the incoming of those of foreign birth and strange tongue and habits for the prosperity of the South, were I permitted I would repeat what I say to my own race, 'Cast down your bucket where you are.' … Cast down your bucket among these people who have, without strikes and labour wars, helped make possible this magnificent representation of the progress of the South. … We shall stand by you with a devotion that no foreigner can approach, ready to lay down our lives, if need be, in defense of yours, interlacing our industrial, commercial, civil, and religious life with yours in a way that shall make the interests of both races one. In all things that are purely social we can be as separate as the fingers, yet one as the hand in all things essential to mutual progress."[3]
—*Booker T. Washington, "The Atlanta Compromise," given at the Cotton States and International Exposition in Atlanta, Georgia, on September 18, 1895*

He was a model example of self-improvement. He would prove to be a valuable teacher at Tuskegee Institute, both instructing and inspiring his students to do their very best despite inequality and adversity.

TEACHING SELF-RELIANCE

Originally only a training facility for elementary school teachers, Tuskegee Institute had quickly added courses in carpentry and blacksmithing. With Carver's arrival, the school would add courses in agricultural science to teach African-American farmers how to best tend the land. Carver's duties included a full teaching load, the administration of the Department of Agriculture, the expansion of the Agricultural Experiment Station, and managing the school's two farms.

All of Carver's work at Tuskegee Institute was done with the goal of reaching poor and uneducated

African Americans. Many of his students had not completed elementary school. Instead of approaching them with a multitude of facts or abstract concepts, Carver taught his students to appreciate nature. He believed that nature provided all of the necessary resources, that nothing was unnecessary or should be wasted, and that everything in nature was interrelated. He showed his students how natural forces worked together to create a single plant. Carver talked about chemistry, botany, and meteorology in terms of farming.

Carver's approach would help poor farmers get by on meager resources. Nature was his classroom. Carver taught his students to collect plant and animal specimens and to study them carefully. He instructed them to categorize their properties and to distinguish those that could be improved by cross-breeding to foster the qualities that would improve their value for the farmer, botanist, or gardener.

In the Agricultural Experiment Station, the research arm of Tuskegee's Department of Agriculture, Carver focused on agricultural methods that were within reach of the poorest of farmers. In part, this was due to the fact that the station was poorly funded. Compared to other, mainly white,

*George Washington Carver with students in his laboratory
at Tuskegee Institute*

teaching institutions, money was in short supply
at Tuskegee Institute. Carver often had to rely on
donations of seeds, fertilizers, and equipment from
friends. Carver's approach was also motivated by his
mission to help poor farmers help themselves.

The traditional focus on cotton farming in
the South had depleted the soil of much needed
nutrients. Cotton removed nutrients from the soil
faster than other crops. Carver experimented with

alternate crops that would return nutrients to the soil rather than remove them. For example, legumes add nitrogen to the soil, making it stronger. Peanuts, sweet potatoes, alfalfa, black-eyed peas, and soybeans are all natural fertilizers. Natural fertilizers were less expensive than chemical fertilizers. Carver thought natural fertilizers would result in healthier crops than chemical fertilizers. Alternating crops such as peanuts and other legumes was meant to provide an income for farmers while allowing the soil to recover. This practice is known as crop rotation. Also, growing edible plants allowed farmers to feed themselves on their crops. This helped them be self-sufficient rather than rely on purchased goods.

"The Greatest Good to the Greatest Number of 'My People'"

The results of Carver's experiments were published in bulletins that were distributed outside of Tuskegee Institute. Carver wrote 44 bulletins that gave valuable practical tips on farming methods, ways to use crops for personal use, and marketing crops and their products to the consumer. The bulletins were very popular in rural areas throughout the South.

Jesup Agricultural Wagon

Carver's work with poor, illiterate African-American farmers in the South began with trips to the country on weekends. He often talked to people after church. These talks were effective but limited in their reach. A new method was needed to reach as many of these farmers as possible. Iowa State College introduced the "movable school" in 1904 with its "Seed Corn Gospel Trains," teaching farmers at railroad stations.

That same year, Carver proposed a wagon to do similar work. He submitted a proposal that included a drawing of a wagon that would carry dairy equipment and educational charts about farming procedures. Carver also suggested lectures. Funding from Morris K. Jesup and the John F. Slater Fund made the proposal reality. The Jesup Agricultural Wagon started as a movable school on May 24, 1906. During its first summer, the wagon reached more than 2,000 people each month.

Beginning in 1892, Tuskegee Institute had invited farmers and teachers from around Alabama for a yearly conference. Carver made these yearly conferences so popular that eventually he offered them on a monthly basis to accommodate the increase in enrollment. In 1904, he began offering A Short Course on Agriculture during the winter months. Farmers were least busy during these months. The course was opened to those not enrolled in regular programs at the school. By 1912, the extension program had enrolled 1,500 students.

The need to travel to Tuskegee prohibited many poor farmers from attending the winter courses. Therefore, Carver traveled around the countryside, teaching farmers where they lived. The demands on Carver's time were overwhelming. Rather than give up reaching farmers too far or too poor to attend

The Jesup Agricultural Wagon later became the Booker T. Washington Agricultural School on Wheels. The movable school helped bring agricultural education to farmers.

Tuskegee Institute, Washington came up with the idea to take the school to them. With financial help from New York banker and philanthropist Morris K. Jesup, the school's agricultural students built and equipped a wagon following Carver's specifications, the Jesup Agricultural Wagon. A member of Carver's department faculty then delivered demonstrations throughout the South based on Carver's curriculum.

News of the extension program traveled quickly. Carver's curriculum soon became a model for many other schools' extension programs. Carver was in demand as a guest speaker at conferences throughout the South. ⌐

105 Peanut Recipes

Carver's bulletin 31, published in June 1925, included 105 recipes for peanuts. Recipes were for sweet and salty concoctions, including cakes, cookies, candy, soups, and sandwiches. Following is one of Carver's soup recipes from that bulletin:

NO. 2, PEANUT SOUP
NUMBER TWO

Take roasted peanuts; grind or mash real fine; to every half a pint add a quart of milk, half a teaspoon salt, 1 saltspoon pepper, 1 small onion minced very fine, 1 bay leaf, 1 stalk of celery chopped very fine or a saltspoon celery seed. Cook for 15 minutes. Great care must be exercised to keep from burning.

Moisten 1 tablespoon of corn starch in a quarter cup of cold milk; add to the soup; stir until thick and smooth; strain through a fine sieve, and serve with peanut wafers.[4]

BULLETIN NO. 31

JUNE 1925

How to Grow the Peanut and 105 Ways of Preparing it for Human Consumption

Seventh Edition
January 1940

By
GEORGE W. CARVER, M. S. in AGR.
Director

EXPERIMENTAL STATION
TUSKEGEE INSTITUTE
Tuskegee Institute, Alabama

Carver published free, easy-to-read agricultural bulletins to share farming information with local farmers, teachers, and housewives.

Because of lack of funds, Carver furnished his first lab with whatever he could find at Tuskegee Institute's junkyard that might be useful.

A Creative Scientist

Carver's significance as a scientist is not based on any one discovery or invention. Carver was a generalist. He combined chemistry, botany, and agricultural sciences. The importance of Carver and his work is that he created usable products from items others often ignored or simply discarded. He was a gifted, creative scientist with a perspective that was intended to help poor farmers.

A Lab, but No Money

Money was scarce at Tuskegee Institute. When Carver arrived in 1896, his laboratory at the Agricultural Experiment Station had almost no budget. He was forced to go to the school's junkyard to furnish his laboratory. Carver used an old desk as a table and discarded bottles, cans, and kitchen utensils as equipment. He worked with the resources available.

Carver studied the water and soil in and around Tuskegee to learn what would grow best in the environment. He experimented with natural and organic fertilizers in an effort to free farmers from buying chemically produced products. He studied indigenous crops and plants to provide viable alternatives to cotton. He built on the study of fungi he had started at Iowa State College to help farmers keep their crops healthy. He examined the nutritional qualities of

"The primary idea in all of my work was to help the farmer and fill the poor man's empty dinner pail. ... My idea is to help the 'man farthest down,' this is why I have made every process just as simply as I could to put it within his reach."[1]

—*George Washington Carver*

Cotton was a favorite crop in the South.

food. Whatever Carver did as a research scientist, he did with practical goals in mind.

Organic Industrial Products

Carver's research was never intended to be an end in itself, but very much a means to an end. He published his formulas and recipes in bulletins distributed to the poor and often uneducated farmers. Carver likely simplified scientific concepts to make them useful. His goal was less to patent his inventions and findings and more to provide farmers with very useful tips. There are only three patents in Carver's name. The Carver Products Company, founded in 1923 with the support of several white businessmen, commercialized his organic products, but none of his patents was ever mass-produced.

Carver's patents exemplify his unique contribution to science. He found ways to use naturally abundant resources to organically create a variety of products, including paints and stains from the clay soil and cosmetics from peanuts and clay. To him, the peanut, the sweet potato, and the soybean were not inferior to cotton, which had long been the favorite southern crop. Carver believed these were viable crop alternatives with unlimited possibilities, as his many creations demonstrate.

Crop Rotation

Though it was the favorite crop in the South, cotton farming had its challenges. Southern soil had been depleted by the almost exclusive farming of cotton. Cotton farming was extremely labor intensive. The boll weevil, a beetle that feeds on

Educating Farmers

Because many farmers were uneducated, they were illiterate and could not read Carver's bulletins. Carver tried to reach these farmers through other means, including farmers' conferences, fair exhibitions, and speeches held at churches and schools.

cotton buds, was a widely spread plague in the South that endangered many harvests. Southern farmers needed alternative crops that would be less harmful to the soil, easier to harvest, and tolerant to pests. Such crops also had to offer marketing possibilities that would make it worthwhile for farmers to rotate them with cotton.

NUTRITION

Carver's most popular bulletin, *How to Grow the Peanut and 105 Ways of Preparing it for Human Consumption,* was also a source for marketing

---

The History of Peanut Butter

George Washington Carver did not invent peanut butter. A crude form of peanut butter prepared as a stew from crushed peanuts first appeared in the fifteenth century in Africa and China. However, it took until the end of the nineteenth century before a process for preparing nut meal was patented by John Harvey and W.K. Kellogg in 1895. Peanut butter was smooth but not very flavorful because the peanuts were steamed rather than roasted before they were ground.

In 1903, Carver began researching the peanut, collecting more than 100 uses for the legume. A somewhat gritty peanut butter was first sold at the Louisiana Purchase Exposition (World's Fair) in St. Louis in 1904 at C.H. Sumner's concession stand. The Krema Products Company in Columbus, Ohio, began mass-producing peanut butter in 1908. It is the oldest peanut butter company still in operation. The creamy peanut butter we know today was made possible by a churning process developed by Joseph L. Rosefield. He sold the patent to Swift and Company, which began production of Peter Pan peanut butter in 1928. Two years later, Rosefield began distributing his own peanut butter: Skippy. Procter & Gamble introduced Jif in 1958. Today, the company produces the most peanut butter: more than 250,000 jars every day.

possibilities for farmers. First published in 1916, the publication offered practical peanut farming tips and ways to market peanuts to consumers. Also, the bulletin listed dozens of food recipes that use peanuts.

Carver also studied the nutritional value of food. He firmly believed that healthy nutrition had medicinal value. Studying the food provided to Tuskegee Institute students, Carver found that certain foods and their ingredients made people sleepy, while others provided energy. Like his other research, Carver used his nutritional findings to educate poor farmers and to help improve their quality of life. In several bulletins, Carver wrote,

Recipes and Formulas

Carver's accomplishments include recipes and formulas for improvements on adhesives, axle grease, bleach, buttermilk, chili sauce, dyes, ink, fuel briquettes, mayonnaise, meat tenderizer, paper, linoleum, instant coffee, metal polish, pavement, shaving cream, plastic, synthetic rubber, shoe polish, talcum powder, and wood stain. All of these products were based on natural ingredients.

fresh fruits … will go a long way toward keeping us healthy … those who partake in fruits and vegetables every day have the clearest minds and the strongest and healthiest bodies … if we eat plenty of good food … we shall not get so tired and weary and shall not have to consult the doctor so often, and pay out such heavy doctor bills. [2]

CHEMURGY

In addition to focusing on the nutritional value of foods, Carver worked for decades on turning agricultural raw materials into industrial products. This discipline would eventually be dubbed "chemurgy." His promotion of the peanut as a natural alternative to other products drew the attention of the white elite, including Henry Ford. The car manufacturer was looking for alternative sources to fuel his successful mass-produced cars.

Carver always worked toward bettering the lives of all people, especially African Americans, through his research and teaching. However, while his time at Tuskegee Institute was abundant with achievements, it was not without challenges. ⌐

Chemurgy

Chemurgy is a branch of chemistry that focuses on producing industrial products from agricultural raw materials. Although the concept had been rather well developed in the early twentieth century by scientists such as Carver, the term itself was not used until 1934. William J. Hale's *The Farm Chemurgi* popularized the concept. In the 1930s, the field of study received support from financiers such as Henry Ford, yet it was not until World War II that chemurgy celebrated its first successes. When the supply of rubber to the United States was cut off during the war, chemurgists used corn to create synthetic rubber. The increase of chemical materials from petroleum in the 1950s caused the decline of chemurgy. The Chemurgic Council disbanded in 1977. George Washington Carver is the most famous representative in this field of science.

Henry Ford, left, was interested in Carver's chemurgy work because he wanted to find alternative car fuels.

Carver, center, and his colleagues at Tuskegee Institute

TENSIONS AT
TUSKEGEE INSTITUTE

W hen George Washington Carver accepted Booker T. Washington's job offer to teach at Tuskegee Institute, he did not imagine the school would be his home for the rest of his life. Several times, Carver was ready to leave the school. Like most homes, his was not without tensions.

Carver had never lived in the South before moving to Alabama. He had been raised by a white family in the Midwest, had attended mostly white schools, and had made—and would make—many white friends. Having earned a master's degree from Iowa State College, a previously all-white school, Carver came to Tuskegee Institute expecting special treatment. Other faculty members had only bachelor's degrees from African-American institutions— mostly Hampton Institute. Some faculty members had no college degree. White schools were usually better equipped and their teachers better trained and paid than their African-American counterparts. His attitude did not make Carver many friends. He complained about his accommodations, requesting a second room for his equipment when most other faculty had to share a single room.

Hampton Institute

Booker T. Washington and many of Carver's colleagues had attended Hampton Institute. Hampton Normal Agricultural Institute was founded in 1868 in southeastern Virginia by Samuel Chapman Armstrong. Established during the Reconstruction period following the Civil War, the school was one of the first colleges for blacks. The school also focused on Native Americans, creating an education program for that specific group in 1878 that lasted for more than four decades.

The school became Hampton University in 1984. Today, the school has more than 5,700 students who study a variety of subjects at the undergraduate and graduate levels.

His salary was almost double that of other faculty, which made him an outsider from the start.

Tuskegee Institute

Tuskegee Normal and Industrial Institute was conceived by Lewis Adam and George Campbell. Adam was a former slave; Campbell was a former slave owner. Both were concerned that the newly freed slaves would not be able to support themselves unless they learned marketable job skills.

The school began with a state grant of $2,000 and a search for the right principal. Booker T. Washington became that principal. Washington was a former slave who had worked his way through a formal education with menial jobs.

On July 4, 1881, the school opened its doors on grounds borrowed from a church. It was originally conceived as a school for teachers but expanded its courses quickly to include industrial and agricultural training. Over the years, Washington was able to attract wealthy white businessmen and philanthropists to Tuskegee Institute, including Andrew Carnegie, John D. Rockefeller, and Julius Rosenwald.

Today, the university consists of five schools that offer courses in arts, sciences, agriculture, business, education, engineering, architecture, nursing, and veterinary medicine. Tuskegee University is considered one of America's top colleges.

GREAT EXPECTATIONS

Washington had hired Carver because he was the only African-American scholar with a graduate degree in agricultural science and the necessary expertise and talent to take over the varied responsibilities of Tuskegee Institute's Department of Agriculture. Washington was determined to have an all-black faculty at the school. He

wanted to make it a premier teaching
school in order to provide a first-rate
education to the African-American
students who enrolled and to the
African-American farmers who
took advantage of the extension
program. He wanted African-
American parents who did not want
their children taught by whites to
have a college to attend. Washington
also strived to improve the school's
image. He wanted to prove that an
African-American school was just as
good as a white school. As a result,
many educational tools became
promotional tools. For example,
Carver's bulletins summarizing his findings at the
Agricultural Experiment Station were meant to
teach farmers and make the school's name known
outside the institute. The better the school's image,
the more support Washington could garner from
the state government, the federal government, and
private benefactors among white industrialists and
philanthropists. So, while the bulletins were meant
to educate readers, they were also intended to attract

> "We are brothers, all
> of us, no matter what
> race or color or con-
> dition, children of the
> same Heavenly Father.
> We rise together or we
> fall together."[1]
> —*Booker T. Washington*

Tuskegee Institute in 1881, the year it was founded

supporters.

Carver was expected to publish a certain number of bulletins each year. He was responsible for researching their content and then writing, typing, and submitting them for printing. Carver was essentially a one-man operation due to the small budget of the Agricultural Experiment Station. Washington placed high demands on Carver. Washington once criticized Carver because he felt that Carver's department was not "doing justice to the matter of getting out the Bulletins."[2] Carver demanded a stenographer to transcribe his dictation. Washington reluctantly granted the request. Another time, Carver was told there was no money left in his budget to print one of the bulletins. Carver demanded an investigation because he was sure he had not spent the meager budget. The investigation revealed that other departments had used Carver's funds. Whether this was done by mistake or on purpose is hard to say. Regardless, Carver did not have much support among the school's faculty.

A Rivalry

This lack of support became clear when the school's poultry yard did not perform well financially. The poultry yard fell under the Department of Agriculture and was Carver's responsibility. In addition

Notorious Study

In 1932, the U.S. Health Service began working with the Tuskegee Institute on a medical study. Six hundred African-American men—399 with syphilis and 201 without—from the Tuskegee area participated. The study became notorious because it denied treatment to the men infected with syphilis, a disease that can result in blindness, heart abnormalities, mental disorders, neurological problems, and death. The study lasted 40 years. During that time, researchers continued to deny treatment to infected participants without informing them of the health risks of participating in the study.

The study ended in 1972 following a leak to the press. A lawsuit was filed in 1973 on behalf of the study's participants and their families. The two groups reached a settlement the following year that included $10 million, lifetime medical benefits, and burial benefits. In 1975, this was expanded to include the wives, widows, and children of the study participants.

to supplying food for students, faculty, and staff, the poultry yard was supposed to be a teaching tool, a promotional tool, and a means for making money. While it succeeded in the first three goals, the poultry yard did not bring in money. This earned Carver criticism from the school's superintendent of industries, John H. Washington, Booker T. Washington's half-brother. New faculty member George R. Bridgeforth also criticized Carver, claiming that Carver was mismanaging the poultry yard. Bridgeforth also claimed that he could run the Department of Agriculture more efficiently than Carver. John H. Washington had found an ally in his attempt to take Carver's power.

Bridgeforth continuously challenged Carver. The two men feuded considerably. In another incident, one of Carver's subordinates claimed that Carver had asked him to submit false reports about the poultry yard. Booker T. Washington's confidence in Carver was shaken. Carver denied the claim. Knowing that Carver was in a vulnerable position, Bridgeforth and other department faculty submitted a reorganization plan for the department. Carver submitted a letter of resignation to Washington, but Washington refused to accept it. The department was reorganized and responsibilities were divided between Bridgeforth and Carver. Carver was put in charge of the Agricultural Experiment Station and all educational endeavors. He continued to oversee the poultry yard. Bridgeforth was eventually named head of the Department of Agricultural Industries and made equal to Carver, whose title was changed to Director of Agricultural Industries and Experiment Station.

"In these strenuous times, we are likely to become morbid and look constantly upon the dark side of life, and spend entirely too much time considering and brooding over what we can't do, rather than what we can do, and instead of growing morose [sullen] and despondent [hopeless] over opportunities either real or imaginary that are shut from us, let us rejoice at the many unexplored fields in which there is unlimited fame and fortune to the successful explorer and upon which there is no color line; simply the survival of the fittest."[3]
—*George Washington Carver*
"A New Industry for Colored Men and Women"
Colored American, January 1908

Underappreciated and Overworked

Though he continued to teach and conduct research at Tuskegee Institute, Carver's relationship with Booker T. Washington was damaged. Carver felt underappreciated and overworked. Gradually, Washington reduced Carver's teaching responsibilities. This allowed Carver to focus on the experiment station and his research into organically-based industrial products. He had more time to follow his new responsibilities as a school representative. By 1915, the success of the extension program and the distribution of the bulletins had made Carver a local celebrity and a highly sought-after speaker. This was merely the beginning of Carver's fame. ⌒

"I am trying to get our people to see that their color does not hold them back as much as they think."[4]

—George Washington Carver

George Washington Carver

George Washington Carver, 1939

A SHINING STAR

ooker T. Washington died on November
15, 1915. Carver was devastated by
Washington's death. The two men had shared
the belief that "education is the key to unlock the
golden door of freedom to our people."[1] Despite

their bickering, they had shared the cause "to help the farmer and fill the poor man's empty dinner pail … to help the 'man farthest down.'"[2] Carver wrote of his regret that "Mr. Washington never knew how much I loved him, and the cause for which he gave his life."[3] Washington's death left an immeasurable void at Tuskegee Institute.

Robert Russa Moton took Washington's position as principal. However, he was not the inspiring spokesperson Washington had been. He was not a public relations expert who could attract the attention of benefactors and financiers. By the time Moton arrived in Tuskegee, Carver was already a local celebrity. Moton soon decided that Carver would also do well at promoting the school.

CARVER'S NEW ROLE

Carver may not have been

Robert Russa Moton

Robert Russa Moton was born in Amelia County, Virginia, on August 26, 1867. He graduated from Hampton Institute in 1890. That same year, he was put in charge of military discipline at the school. He held the position for 25 years. Moton left Hampton in 1915 to succeed Booker T. Washington as principal of Tuskegee Institute. The school expanded physically and academically under Moton's leadership.

Moton received several honors in his later years. When the Lincoln Memorial was dedicated in Washington, D.C., on May 30, 1922, Moton was one of the speakers. He received the Harmon Award in Race Relations in 1930 and the Spingarn Medal of the National Association for the Advancement of Colored People in 1932. In addition, he was awarded honorary degrees from many schools, including Harvard University and Howard University.

popular among his colleagues, but
he was extremely popular with his
students and the farmers who took
advantage of the school's extension
program and Carver's bulletins.
Moton recognized this and celebrated
Carver's achievements in many of the
school's public relations pamphlets.
Carver was a powerful marketing
asset.

Carver's status on campus grew.
His national and international
reputation increased as well. Carver
was honored for his work as a scientist
and as an artist. In 1916, Carver
was invited to join the advisory
board of the National Agricultural
Society because of his efforts to
address wartime food shortages.
This followed an invitation in 1915
to become a member of the Royal
Society for the Encouragement of the
Arts, Manufactures, and Commerce
because of his accomplishments as
a painter. This invitation became

A Royal Society

The Royal Society for the
Encouragement of the
Arts, Manufactures, and
Commerce is a British
institution based in
London. The organiza-
tion honors and advances
several disciplines in the
arts. Founded in 1754,
numerous notable fig-
ures have been members,
including Karl Marx, Ben-
jamin Franklin, Adam
Smith, Charles Dickens,
and George Washington
Carver.

popular material for newspaper articles on Carver that told the story of the former slave's rise to become a member of a royal society.

THE MAKING OF A LEGEND

Like Booker T. Washington, Carver was adept at advancing the African-American cause without offending white benefactors. He dispelled many white men's notion that African Americans were inferior to whites. He drew attention to and gained support for Tuskegee Institute from a variety of people, including those in high positions.

When World War I started in 1914, the U.S. government developed interest in alternate food sources for shortages created because of strained relationships with European nations. In January 1918, the U.S. Department of Agriculture (USDA) invited Carver to Washington, D.C., to explore the possibility of using the sweet potato as a replacement for wheat. The end of the war brought an end to this particular project, but Carver's relationship with the USDA continued.

Carver developed a process for making peanut milk. Enthusiastic about its possibilities, he contacted the United Peanut Association of America.

Because peanut milk had already been patented, this brought an end to the project, but he did establish an important relationship. In 1920, the United Peanut Association of America invited Carver to address its convention in Montgomery, Alabama. His speech on the possibilities of the peanut dazzled the predominantly white audience. Ironically, Carver used the freight elevator to get to the stage because segregation laws reserved the passenger elevators for whites only.

On that day, Carver convinced many influential white representatives of the peanut industry that he was not inferior. From there, it was but a short step to speaking before the Ways and Means Committee of

The USDA

The USDA was established as part of the Agricultural Act signed by Abraham Lincoln on May 15, 1862. The USDA's programs and services span seven areas represented by its branches:

- Natural Resources and Environment
- Farm and Foreign Agricultural Services
- Rural Development
- Food, Nutrition, and Consumer Services
- Food Safety
- Research, Education, and Economics
- Marketing and Regulatory Program

The USDA's mission is to "provide leadership on food, agriculture, natural resources, and related issues based on sound public policy, the best available science, and efficient management." The USDA's vision is "to be recognized as a dynamic organization that is able to efficiently provide the integrated program delivery needed to lead a rapidly evolving food and agriculture system."[4]

the U.S. House of Representatives on behalf of the United Peanut Association of America in support of a tariff on imported peanuts. In 1921, shortly after his presentation to the Ways and Means Committee, the U.S. government imposed the tariff Carver supported. This action was yet another validation of Carver's knowledge and ability.

The attention that had begun when Carver became a member of the Royal Society for the Encouragement of the Arts, Manufactures, and Commerce continued. The story of his rise from slave to internationally renowned scientist was repeated in numerous publications. Carver enjoyed the fame and recognition. Tuskegee Institute was not at all hesitant about capitalizing on Carver's reputation. Carver attended many official functions, conventions, and exhibitions with the purpose of luring investors to the South in general and to Tuskegee in particular.

Another Prominent Peanut Man

U.S. history has seen another prominent peanut man since George Washington Carver. James (Jimmy) Earl Carter ran his family's peanut farm from 1953 to 1962, when he became active as a Democratic member of the Georgia Senate. Carter was president of the United States from 1977 to 1981. Today, like Carver, he works to better the lives of others through his nonprofit organization, the Carter Center, and Habitat for Humanity.

His accomplishments as a scientist and educator and his skill with people were indisputable. Still, while he liked and appreciated the attention and accolades, the work that made Carver most proud was teaching poor African-American farmers about agriculture. ⌐

Carver developed a variety of products from peanuts, including oil, flour, candy, and animal feed.

Carver's work attracted prominent white businessmen, such as Henry Ford, left, and his son, Edsel, right.

BRIDGING TROUBLED WATERS

arver's rise to fame was as much due to his willingness and ability to accept the status quo as it was to his scientific and educational achievements. He never endorsed segregation, yet he never publicly spoke out against it. Like Booker

T. Washington, Carver did not believe that it was necessary or helpful to challenge whites. Most of Tuskegee Institute's benefactors and many of his best friends were white.

A ROLE MODEL

Race relations were important to Carver. He considered it his God-given duty to do his part to improve them. Political activism, however, did not suit Carver's personality. Instead, he wanted to be a role model for other African Americans. Carver viewed his life as proof that hard work and diligence could lead to success, regardless of the color of one's skin. Carver believed a color-blind society would emerge only if more and more African Americans disproved the racist beliefs of white supremacists through the achievements in their own lives.

In 1923, an exhibit in Atlanta, Georgia, showcased his work. Carver received a letter of endorsement from the Atlanta Chapter of the United Daughters of the Confederacy (UDC). The UDC was a conservative white organization dedicated to the preservation of the memory of the role of the South during the Civil War. Expressing an appreciation for Carver's work was meant to show

that the organization in particular
and the South in general were not as
racist as the rest of the United States
and the world seemed to think. At
the same time, the fact that there
was an African-American man with
honorable achievements was meant
to show that the policy of racial
segregation so deeply engrained
in the South did not, in fact,
suppress the advancement of African
Americans. The accomplishments
of men such as Carver were used to
prove that the policy of separate but
equal worked just fine.

In the same year, 1923, Carver
received the Spingarn Medal,
an award given by the National
Association for the Advancement
of Colored People (NAACP).
Founded in 1909 as an alternative
to Booker T. Washington's policies
of accommodation, the NAACP
was regarded by many as a somewhat
radical organization that actively

The UDC

The United Daughters of
the Confederacy (UDC)
was founded in 1894 to
commemorate those who
served and died for the
Confederacy during the
American Civil War. The
UDC's objectives are to
preserve the history of
the South as it pertains
to the Civil War and to
aid the education of de-
scendants of Confederate
soldiers. The organization
has been accused of hav-
ing a white supremacist
agenda. Membership is
open to any woman
over the age of 16 who
is a descendant of a
Confederate soldier.

promoted social and political change. It fought court battles aimed at overturning the Jim Crow statutes that had been signed into law as methods for legalizing segregation.

The Spingarn Medal was an annual award honoring those considered to have worked most toward advancing the African-American race. Carver received the medal because of his achievements in agricultural chemistry and his instrumental role in increasing interracial understanding. The NAACP recognized that Carver could advance the organization's cause without offending the white establishment.

Carver's achievements and growing celebrity made him a regular presence on the lecture circuit throughout the South—and not only before African Americans. His audiences included both African Americans and whites.

The NAACP

The NAACP was founded in 1909 by a diverse group of civil rights activists, including Henry Moscovitz, a Jewish social worker, William E. Walling, the son of a former slave-owning family, and W.E.B. DuBois, a great African-American writer and thinker. The NAACP's first focus was to overturn the Jim Crow laws that legalized segregation and racial discrimination and to stop lynching.

In the 1930s, Thurgood Marshall became head of the organization's legal arm and helped win the 1954 Supreme Court case *Brown v. Board of Education*, which desegregated public schools. Marshall was appointed to the Supreme Court by President Johnson in 1967 and held the post until 1991. Other famous members of the NAACP include Rosa Parks, whose refusal to give up her seat on a bus in Montgomery, Alabama, prompted the bus boycott in that city in 1955, and civil rights activist Jesse Jackson.

The CIC

The Commission on Interracial Integration (CIC) was founded in Atlanta, Georgia, in 1919. The CIC developed out of activities by multiple organizations that worked toward easing racial tensions, including the YMCA War Work Council and the Atlanta Christian Council. The CIC opposed lynching and mob brutality. The CIC also worked to educate white southerners about racial abuse. In addition to the main office in Atlanta, there were state committees and approximately 800 local interracial committees. Rather than simply attack segregation, the CIC strived to "bring together the 'best people' of both races to discuss racial problems."[1] The CIC merged with the Southern Regional Council in 1944.

Reaching Out to the Younger Generation

Perhaps Carver's greatest accomplishment with race relations was his ability to inspire admiration among younger generations, regardless of skin color. Carver's speeches rarely addressed race relations directly. Instead, he would focus on his scientific achievements and ways to use them and those of others to improve the South's economy. His message was that African Americans were able to think innovatively and progressively. They were, as Booker T. Washington had put it, willing participants in revitalizing the South for the mutual benefit of both races. Supported by the Young Men's Christian Association (YMCA) and the Commission on Interracial Cooperation (CIC), Carver spread his message in countless lectures before young audiences of both races.

Many of the young people he met at such lectures became part of what he called his family. Carver never married nor had children. Instead, he adopted young minds along his way as a teacher and lecturer, corresponding with them for the rest of his life. Some of these young people wrote letters to Carver in which they addressed him as "Dad." It was through the cultivation of such personal contacts that Carver was able to inspire African Americans and whites alike to seek out similarly peaceful ways of

The YMCA

The YMCA began in London, England, on June 6, 1844, in response to changes that occurred in big cities as a result of the Industrial Revolution. Many young men moved from the country to cities, working 10 to 12 hours a day, six days a week. Alone and separated from their homes and families, these young men often lived at work. George Williams and fellow employees at a draper's shop formed the first YMCA to provide Bible study and prayer as a replacement for street life.

The first YMCA in the United States was established in Boston, Massachusetts, in 1851. During the American Civil War, the YMCA was committed to helping soldiers and sailors. After the war, it focused on saving men's souls. In the 1880s, YMCAs began creating buildings that would later have gymnasiums, swimming pools, auditoriums, bowling alleys, and dormitories. Eventually, YMCAs started working with boys and organizing summer camps. This expanded to working with college students.

At the end of World War II, more than half of all YMCAs allowed women. Families became the organization's new focus. Today, the YMCA works with anyone, regardless of age, race, religion, or economic status, providing a variety of health and human services. The organization's motto clearly speaks its goal: "We build strong kids, strong families, strong communities."[2]

improving the quality of life for all people.

By the time Carver had become an inspiration to African Americans and whites, he was at an advanced age. Knowing full well how difficult race relations can be, Carver promoted a revolution from within. From the vantage point of a man in his sixties, he firmly believed that the future of the United States lay in convincing younger generations of the true equality of humans, regardless of skin color. ⌐

The USS *George Washington Carver*

The U.S. Navy honored Carver by christening a vessel after him. The USS *George Washington Carver* was a nuclear-powered ballistic submarine. The ship's motto is "Strength through Knowledge."[3] Commissioned in 1966, the vessel operated out of Holy Loch, Scotland, and carried out 73 patrols in the Atlantic Ocean before being decommissioned March 18, 1993, at the Puget Sound Naval Shipyard in Bremerton, Washington, where it resides today.

Carver working in his lab at Tuskegee Institute

George Washington Carver

A MAN OF GREAT FAITH

arver was driven by his desire to serve his race. Carver thought he could best do this by sharing his knowledge of agriculture, botany, and other subjects with others. And his knowledge, he believed, came to him by divine inspiration. Carver believed that God revealed Himself in His creation. The wonders of nature were proof to Carver that God was everywhere.

BREAKING DOWN BARRIERS

Considering that Carver was a scientist, such beliefs are surprising. Reasoning and deduction are major principles of the scientific endeavor. To Carver, however, science and religious devotion were not contradictory. Religion had always played a major role in his life. It sometimes broke down social and racial barriers. At church services, prayer groups, and Bible circles, Carver made friends with people who shared his religious convictions. On common ground before God, many of the whites he met were able to see beyond his race. Skin color and economic status did not matter. Before God, everyone was equal. While at Iowa State College, where

"Never since have I been without this consciousness of the Creator speaking to me through flowers, rocks, animals, plants, and all other aspects of His creation."[1]
—*George Washington Carver*

racial discrimination was common, Carver was able to create a place for himself among white students by attending prayer groups and joining the YMCA. Throughout his life, religion provided Carver with a home in otherwise hostile environments.

Nature: Perfect Balance and Harmony

Carver saw perfect balance and harmony in nature. Nothing was lacking and nothing was redundant. This was evidence for divine design. As a boy marveling at the beauty of nature in the woods around his home, Carver had admired the intricate relationship of everything he saw: the earth, plants, animals, man, the sun, and the moon. According to Carver, "I literally lived in the woods. I wanted to know every strange stone, flower, insect, bird or beast."[2]

As an adult, Carver often referred to God as "Mr. Creator" and to his

"I never grope for methods. The method is revealed at the moment I am inspired to create something new. I lived in the woods, I wanted to know everything: every strange stone, flower, insect, bird or beast. I gather specimens and listen to what God has to say to me. After I have had my morning talk with God, I go to my laboratory and begin to carry out His wishes for the day."[3]
—*George Washington Carver*
"The Story the Peanut Tells"
Address given in Minneapolis, Minnesota, on April 6, 1938

lab as "God's little workshop." He claimed that, while reading about nature was fine, "if a person walks in the woods and listens carefully, he can learn more than what is in books, for they speak with the voice of God."[4]

Not everyone responded favorably to such statements. At a public speaking engagement in New York City in 1924, Carver referred to inspiration as a source for his research. This provoked a negative editorial titled "Men of Science Never Talk That Way" in the November 19, 1924, issue of the *New York Times*. In the article, Carver was criticized for scorning books and attributing his scientific successes to divine inspiration rather than research and logical deduction through trial and error. The editorial argued that Carver showed a terrible disregard for the accepted methods of science and that men of science

"In the whole life of this saintly man I see the future of a great race. In his eyes I see the soul of a people who experienced God and understand the meaning of the Cross.

The unique contribution George Carver has made in the field of science and religion is symbolical of the contribution the Negro race is destined to make to our civilization if all unequal relationships are abolished and the Negro is given every opportunity fully to develop his personality."[5]
—*Howard Kester in a 1926 letter to Carver*

should never talk that way:

> *Real chemists, or at any rate other real chemists, do not scorn books out of which they can learn what other chemists have done, and they do not ascribe their successes, when they have any, to "inspiration." Talk of that sort simply will bring ridicule on an admirable institution and on the race for which it has done and still is doing so much.* [6]

Carver felt misunderstood. He responded by citing his degrees, listing books in his library that he had read, and arguing fiercely that his scientific methodology was beyond reproach. The *New York Times* never printed Carver's response. However, friends and acquaintances in Christian circles came to his aid, distributing his response in other newspapers.

SCIENCE VERSUS RELIGION

At the time, this debate over religion and science was by no means isolated. The early twentieth century was characterized by discussion about the relationship

---

The Scientific Method

The scientific method relies on research and observations to ask and answer scientific questions. The steps of the method are:

· Ask a question.
· Conduct background research.
· Formulate a hypothesis.
· Test the hypothesis.
· Analyze the data from the experiment and draw a conclusion.
· Communicate the results of the experiment.

Charles Darwin's On the Origin of Species *caused a heated debate over religion and science.*

between religion and science. On March 13, 1925, a few months after the *New York Times* had criticized Carver's inspirational approach to science, the state of Tennessee passed the Butler Act. The law made it illegal to teach "any theory that denies the story of the Divine Creation of man as taught in the Bible, and to teach instead that man has descended from a lower order of animals."[7]

Charles Darwin's *On the Origin of Species,* published in 1859, explained his theory of evolution. Darwin believed all species slowly evolve by the principles of natural selection, or survival of the fittest. Even though man is barely mentioned in *On the Origin of Species,* some religious fundamentalists interpreted evolution as a criticism of the Biblical account of creation. If man evolved over time, God could not have created man in His image. Not everyone thought Darwin's theory contradicted

---

Charles Darwin

Charles Darwin was born on February 12, 1809, in Shrewsbury, England. His father was a successful doctor. Darwin started studying medicine and switched to theology before pursuing botany. After graduating from Cambridge University, he took a sea voyage. During the five-year trip, Darwin studied nature. He put notes together from his experiences and began writing *On the Origin of the Species,* a book he did not publish until he was 50.

Darwin wrote 19 books, the most famous of which was *On the Origin of the Species,* in which he discussed his ideas on evolution. Though he discusses the evolution of a variety of creatures in the book, Darwin never discusses the evolution of man. Even so, the book sparked much debate over science and religion, pitting creationism, the idea that God created everything, including man, against evolution. While many people accepted Darwin's views, many others were angered by his book.

While he did not address the evolution of man in *On the Origin of the Species,* Darwin did write about humans and evolution in *The Descent of Man* and *The Expression of the Emotions.*

Darwin married Emma Wedgewood in 1839. Together more than 40 years, they had ten children. Charles Darwin died on April 19, 1882. He was 73.

religion, but many people debated the issue. *On the Origin of Species* was pitted against the biblical book of Genesis over the one true explanation of the development of life.

A few months after the Butler Act had been signed into law, the famous Scopes Trial took place. During the summer of 1925, Tennessee high school teacher John Scopes defended his right to teach the theory of evolution in the classroom. After eight days of heated arguments by opposing attorneys Clarence Darrow and William Jennings Bryan, the jury took only nine minutes to deliberate. Scopes was found guilty. He was sentenced to a fine and no longer allowed to teach any ideas that might have derived from Darwin's *On the Origin of Species*. Science and religion seemed mutually exclusive. At the time, religion was the favored viewpoint.

"How my very soul goes out to people who have not found the first principle of true happiness and Divine love, which must rule the world."[8]
—*George Washington Carver*

DIVINE INSPIRATION

Carver believed that science and religion were not mutually exclusive. To Carver, there was no conflict between science and religion. He once stated,

> *Nature in its varied forms are the little windows through which God permits me to commune with him, and to see much of His glory, majesty and power by simply lifting the curtain and looking in.*[9]

Carver believed his job as a scientist was not to question God's creation but to decode and decipher God's divine design. Even though divine inspiration did not qualify as an accepted method of scientific research, as the *New York Times* so clearly noted, the incident with the newspaper did not tarnish Carver's reputation as a scientist. To the contrary, the debate fueled his image as a man who stood up for his beliefs despite criticism and adversity. ⌐

The state of Tennessee sued John Scopes, a high school biology teacher, for teaching evolution to his students.

George Washington Carver, 1942

An Inspiration

*G*eorge Washington Carver was a formidable
educator who helped poor African-
American farmers help themselves. He was a scientist
who found creative ways to use natural resources.
He was an artist who eternalized his appreciation

for nature in his many beautiful
paintings of flowers. He was a devout
Christian who dedicated his life to
the service of his people and God.
It is no wonder, then, that the *New
York Times*—the publication that had
criticized him for his unorthodox
scientific methods—dubbed him a
"black Leonardo" in 1941. The paper
likened Carver to Leonardo da Vinci,
the prototype of a Renaissance man, a well-rounded
person talented in many areas, including both
science and art. Like da Vinci, Carver was a gifted
inventor and painter. Also like da Vinci, Carver was
ahead of his time.

> "How far you go in life depends on your being tender with the young, compassionate with the aged, sympathetic with the striving and tolerant of the weak and strong. Because someday in your life you will have been all of these."[1]
>
> —*George Washington Carver*

TEACHING A NATION

After the stock market crash on October 29,
1929, the American economy declined steadily over
a period of several years. The Great Depression was
characterized by high unemployment rates, poverty,
and forced foreclosures, or loss of people's homes
because they could not pay for them. It affected not
only the United Sates. It eventually spread to Europe
and around the world.

Just as Carver had done with the poor farmers at the turn of the century in an attempt to revitalize the South, he now taught an entire destitute country how to get by on next to nothing. He recycled and refreshed his earlier research, focusing on writing about diet, nutrition, and economical ways to feed a family. He promoted self-sufficiency and creative ways to make do with the few resources available.

A Man of Honor

Late in his life, Carver received formal recognition for his lifetime of varied work. In 1928, he was awarded an honorary doctorate of science degree from Simpson College, the school he had once attended. In 1935, Carver became an official consultant for the USDA's plant disease research, reaching back to his graduate work on fungi at Iowa State College. In 1937, Carver became a spokesman for the chemurgy movement, which promoted the cooperation of different scientific disciplines to advance agricultural research as a whole. This was precisely the kind

Because you have opened doors of opportunity to those Americans who happen to be Negroes; because you have once again demonstrated that in human ability there is no color line; because you have helped thousands of men acquire new confidence and self-respect.[2]
—University of Rochester upon conferring an honorary degree upon Carver in 1941

Because of his work, Carver met many prominent people, including President Franklin D. Roosevelt, right.

of interdisciplinary work Carver had pioneered throughout his career at Tuskegee Institute.

These honors continued to bring fame and recognition to Carver. They also brought financial supporters to Tuskegee Institute. In 1939, President Franklin D. Roosevelt visited the school. Carver's talent at making friends in high places also created a lasting relationship with Henry Ford, the automobile innovator. The two men had met in the 1930s at a conference of the chemurgy movement. Ford, in search of alternate ways to produce fuel, was one of the sponsors of the movement. Ford was also an admirer of Carver's early work on organic industrial products. He recognized the potential of Carver's pioneering principle to look to nature first for any and all products.

HELPING POLIO VICTIMS

While in college, Carver had worked as masseur for the football team. Throughout the years, he continued giving massages to friends to help alleviate a variety of ailments. In the 1920s, he began treating a boy with peanut-oil massages. The boy, Foy, was skinny, weak, and anemic. Carver treated Foy three times a week. After a month of treatment, the boy gained more than 30 pounds and became stronger and healthier. Carver believed he had discovered a treatment for polio.

Convinced of the restorative powers of the peanut-oil massages, Carver treated two polio sufferers. The patients experienced positive results that Carver concluded were because of the treatments he administered. Carver began to hint at his discovery in speeches, but a newspaper shared Carver's experience with the world, quoting him

as saying, "It has been given out that I have found a cure. I have not, but it looks hopeful."[3]

Publication of the article prompted numerous requests for peanut-oil treatment from all kinds of people for a variety of ailments. Within weeks, more than 1,100 letters arrived. People went to Tuskegee to request help from Carver in person. Carver took on more than a dozen patients. He also provided detailed instruction of his treatment to some doctors and to individual patients. In 1935, Carver changed the focus of the treatment on the massaging rather than the oil.

In 1939, Tuskegee Institute was granted more than $160,000 by the National Foundation for Infantile Paralysis to create a clinic for crippled children.

Polio

Caused by a virus, polio has three forms:
- abortive polio
- nonparalytic polio
- paralytic polio

People who experience the more common forms of abortive or nonparalytic polio may never realize they have the disease. Symptoms of abortive polio are similar to those of the flu. Symptoms of nonparalytic polio include neck pain and sensitivity to light. When most people think of polio, they think of paralysis, which is caused by the third type of polio. Paralytic polio causes paralysis and even death.

There was a large outbreak of polio in the United States during the first half of the twentieth century. During that time, tens of thousands of cases were reported, mostly among children. In 1955, Jonas Salk introduced a polio vaccination that has almost eliminated the occurrence of the disease in the United States. However, polio still exists in other parts of the world.

CARVER'S LEGACY

While Carver was in his seventies, his work took on a more symbolic nature. With the help of Austin W. Curtis Jr., his assistant and protégé, Carver continued to promote his cause through speaking engagements and appearances on radio shows. Carver had become such a celebrity that in 1940 a Hollywood movie celebrating his life was made and the publisher Doubleday Doran and Company commissioned a biographer to chronicle his life.

Most of Carver's efforts at the end of his life were devoted to the Carver Museum and Foundation at Tuskegee Institute. Tuskegee offered an old laundry building to be converted into a museum. With the financial help of Ford, renovation began in 1938. Over the next few years, Carver supervised the establishment of his own legacy. The museum would showcase the inspirational aspects

Austin W. Curtis Jr.

Austin W. Curtis Jr. graduated from Cornell University with a degree in chemistry. Curtis taught at North Carolina Agricultural and Technical College before accepting the position to work with Carver at Tuskegee Institute. Though he was Carver's assistant, Curtis actually received a higher salary than Carver.

Curtis took over much of the everyday managerial and organizational work Carver had done. Curtis also pursued a few of Carver's earlier ideas and researched some of his own. More than an assistant, Curtis was also a surrogate son to Carver. Shortly after Curtis began working at Tuskegee Institute, Carver wrote to the young man's father that "he seems to me more like a son than a person who had just come to work for me."[4] Curtis even referred to himself as "Baby Carver."

Austin W. Curtis Jr. was a chemist and assistant to George Washington Carver.

of Carver's life and achievements. The foundation would offer scholarships to young scientists. The museum and foundation would ensure that Carver's legacy would survive him.

George Washington Carver died on January 5, 1943, in Tuskegee, Alabama. He was 77 years old. Nothing symbolizes Carver's significance more than the fact that, on July 14, 1943, Congress appropriated $30,000 for the creation of a George

Washington Carver National Monument. Senator Harry S. Truman from Missouri, later president of the United States, recommended the appropriation. Located near Diamond, Missouri, the monument includes a bust of Carver, a museum, and Moses Carver's house from 1881. Carver's was the first national monument celebrating an African American. It is still one of only a few national monuments that honor an individual's birthplace.

Honoring Carver's birthplace reminds Americans of a darker time in U.S. history. It also pays tribute to the struggle of African Americans, a cause always at the forefront of Carver's work. Carver created the life he wanted. He wished for other African Americans to do the same. A skilled scientist, imaginative researcher, gifted teacher, talented painter, and thoughtful leader, Carver contributed to the growth of his students and African-American farmers. More than this, he aided in the survival of countless Americans during the Great Depression. Carver taught by example and wished for others to do the same. ⌒

A statue of a young George Washington Carver sits at the
Carver National Monument in Missouri.

TIMELINE

1864 or 1865

George Washington Carver is born in Diamond Grove, Missouri.

1877

Carver begins his formal education in Neosho, Missouri.

1884

Carver attends high school in Minneapolis, Kansas.

1891

Carver attends Iowa State College of Agricultural and Mechanical Arts.

1893

Carver exhibits a painting at the World's Columbian Exhibition (the World's Fair) in Chicago, Illinois.

1894

Carver becomes a graduate student and a staff member of Iowa State College after receiving his bachelor's degree from the school.

1885	1886	1890
Carver is rejected on the basis of race by Highland College in Kansas.	Carver homesteads in Ness County, Kansas.	Carver enrolls at Simpson College in Iowa.

1896	1898	1916
Carver receives a Master of Agriculture degree from Iowa State College and becomes director of agriculture at Tuskegee Institute.	Carver begins issuing bulletins on his work at Tuskegee Institute's Agricultural Experiment Station.	Carver is named to the advisory board of the National Agricultural Society.

PROFESSOR CARVER'S
First Laboratory

TIMELINE

1918	1919	1921
Carver becomes a consultant in agricultural research for the U.S. Department of Agriculture.	Carver develops peanut milk.	Carver appears before the House Ways and Means Committee January 21 to argue for a tariff on imported peanuts.

1935	1937	1938
Carver works as a consultant to the U.S. Department of Agriculture.	Carver becomes a spokesman at various chemurgy conventions.	*The Story of Dr. Carver* is released on June 19.

1923

Carver is awarded the Spingarn Medal from the NAACP, receives a letter of recognition from the UDC, and founds the Carver Products Company.

1924

A *New York Times* article criticizes Carver's citing of divine inspiration as a method of scientific research.

1928

Carver receives an honorary doctoral degree from Simpson College.

1939

The George Washington Carver Museum opens in Tuskegee, Alabama.

1943

Carver dies on January 5 in Tuskegee, Alabama.

1953

The George Washington Carver National Monument in Diamond, Missouri, opens.

ESSENTIAL FACTS

DATE OF BIRTH
1864 or 1865

PLACE OF BIRTH
Diamond Grove, Missouri

DATE OF DEATH
January 5, 1943

PARENTS
Mother, Mary; father, unknown; foster parents, Moses and Susan Carver

EDUCATION
Simpson College; Iowa State College

MARRIAGE
Never married

CHILDREN
None

RESIDENCES
Missouri, Kansas, Iowa, Alabama

Career Highlights

❖ In 1894, Carver received a master's degree in agriculture from Iowa State College.

❖ In March of 1898, Carver became head of Tuskegee Institute's Department of Agriculture.

❖ In 1923, Carver was awarded the NAACP's Spingarn Medal in honor of his numerous achievements in combating racial and social inequality.

❖ In 1925, Carver patented three methods of producing paints and stains from clay and peanuts.

❖ In 1935, Carver became an official consultant for the USDA's mycology and plant disease research.

Societal Contribution

Carver dedicated his life to inspiring those around him and cultivating ways to improve the lives of those suffering from racial, social, and economic inequalities. He did so through his work as a scientist and as an educator.

Conflicts

Throughout his life, Carver faced many challenges because of racial prejudice and inequality. Carver also experienced tension with faculty at Tuskegee Institute who felt he behaved as if he were superior to them.

Quote

"How far you go in life depends on your being tender with the young, compassionate with the aged, sympathetic with the striving and tolerant of the weak and strong. Because someday in your life you will have been all of these."—*George Washington Carver*

ADDITIONAL RESOURCES

SELECT BIBLIOGRAPHY

Adair, Gene. *George Washington Carver*. New York: Chelsea House Publishers, 1989.

Benge, Janet, and Geoff Benge. *George Washington Carver: From Slave to Scientist*. Seattle, WA: YWAM Publishing, 2001.

Brandenberg, Aliki. *A Weed Is a Flower: The Life of George Washington Carver*. New York: Aladdin Paperbacks, 1988.

Burchard, Peter. *Carver: A Great Soul*. Fairfax, CA: Serpent Wise, 1998.

Holt, Rackham. *George Washington Carver: An American Biography*. New York: Doubleday, 1943.

McMurry, Linda O. *George Washington Carver: Scientist and Symbol*. New York: Oxford, 1981.

FURTHER READING

Collins, David. *George Washington Carver: Man's Slave Becomes God's Scientist*. New York: Mott Media, 1981.

Driscoll, Laura. *George Washington Carver: Peanut Wizard*. New York: Grosset and Dunlap, 2003.

Kremer, Gary R. *George Washington Carver: In His Own Words*. Columbia, MO: University of Missouri Press, 1987.

Web Links

To learn more about George Washington Carver, visit ABDO Publishing Company on the World Wide Web at **www.abdopublishing.com**. Web sites about George Washington Carver are featured on our Book Links page. These links are routinely monitored and updated to provide the most current information available.

Places To Visit

George Washington Carver Museum and Cultural Center
1165 Angelina Street, Austin, TX 78702
512-974-4926
www.austincityconnection.com/carver/history.htm
This site includes exhibits about African-American scientists and inventors, the African-American celebration Juneteenth, and Austin, Texas, African-American families.

George Washington Carver National Monument
5646 Carver Road, Diamond, MO 64840
417-325-4151
www.nps.gov/gwca
This national park offers the Carver Science Discovery Center, where visitors can participate in lab experiments. Exhibits at the Carver Boyhood Diarama depict Carver's life as a child. Explore the outdoors Carver enjoyed on the Carver Nature Trail.

Tuskegee Institute National Historic Site
1212 West Montgomery Road, Tuskegee Institute, AL 36088
334-727-3200
www.nps.gov/tuin
Located on the campus of Tuskegee Institute, this National Historic Site includes the George Washington Carver Museum and Booker T. Washington's home. The site also offers an interactive virtual exhibit titled "Legends of Tuskegee."

Glossary

botany
> A branch of biology that focuses on the study of plant life.

chemistry
> The science that examines composition, structure, properties, and reactions of matter.

chemurgy
> A field of applied chemistry that deals with creating industrial products from agricultural raw materials.

crop rotation
> A system of farming in which different crops are planted on the same land in successive years rather than the same crop year after year. Crop rotation helps prevent depletion of the soil's nutrients.

ecology
> The science that studies the interrelationship of organisms and their environments.

evolution
> The change of the characteristics of a species over time. The theory of evolution was developed by Charles Darwin in the mid-nineteenth century and holds that the process of natural selection will change a species over time, developing only those traits that are advantageous to survival of the entire species.

homestead
> Land obtained from the U.S. government by filing a record, living on the land, and cultivating it; the land and the buildings on it.

Jim Crow laws
> State and local laws in Southern and border states that legalized segregation between the 1880s and 1960s.

legume
> The edible fruit or seed of plants, including peas, beans, and peanuts.

mycology
>   An area of biology that focuses on the study of fungi.

National Association for the Advancement of Colored People (NAACP)
>   An American organization established in the early twentieth century that strives for the betterment of African Americans and other people of color.

racism
>   The practice of bigotry, prejudice, violence, oppression, stereotyping, discrimination, or segregation based on race.

Reconstruction
>   Reorganization of the Southern states following the American Civil War.

segregation
>   The separation of people based on race, gender, class, or ethnicity.

sharecropping
>   The farming practice common in the South following the Civil War. Poor farmers were given part of the proceeds of the sale of crops they planted and harvested in exchange for using the land they worked. The system developed out of landowners' inability to pay much in wages and now-free slaves being illiterate, poor, and in need of work.

slavery
>   The act of holding people against their will, depriving them of their freedoms, and making them work for no pay.

Source Notes

Chapter 1. A Dazzling Performance
1. Linda O. McMurry. *George Washington Carver: Scientist and Symbol.* New York: Oxford University Press, 1981. 172.
2. Ibid. 173–174.
3. Ibid. 27.

Chapter 2. A Thirst for Knowledge
1. Linda O. McMurry. *George Washington Carver: Scientist and Symbol.* New York: Oxford University Press, 1981. 26–27.
2. Ibid. 40.
3. Ibid. 41.
4. Gale Group, Inc. "George Washington Carver." 2001. 29 Oct. 2007 <http://www.africawithin.com/bios/george_carver.htm>.
5. George Washington Carver. "To Booker T. Washington." 12 Apr. 1896, *Booker T. Washington Papers.* Vol. 4. Champaign, IL: University of Illinois Press, 2000. 159. 12 July 2007 <http://www.historycooperative.org/btw/Vol.4/html/159.html>.

Chapter 3. A Formidable Teacher
1. "Remembering Jim Crow: Jim Crow Laws." *American RadioWorks.* American Public Media. 2007. 25 July 2007 <http://americanradioworks.publicradio.org/features/remembering/laws.html>.
2. Booker T. Washington. "Atlanta Compromise." Cotton States and International Exposition. Atlanta. 18 Sept. 1895. 13 July 2007 <http://historymatters.gmu.edu/d/39/>.
3. Ibid.
4. George Washington Carver. "How to Grow the Peanut and 105 Ways of Preparing it for Human Consumption," *Experimental Station Bulletin* June 1925. PLANTanswers.com. Texas A&M University. 29 Oct. 2007, <http://plantanswers.tamu.edu/recipes/peanutrecipes.html>.

Chapter 4. A Creative Scientist

1. The National Park Service. *George Washington Carver National Monument*. 13 July 2007 <http://www.nps.gov/archive/gwca/ expanded/quotes_2.htm>.

2. Peter Duncan Burchard. *George Washington Carver: For His Time and Ours*. Diamond, Missouri: George Washington Monument, 2005. 138–139.

Chapter 5. Tensions at Tuskegee Institute

1. The National Park Service. "Carver Quotes." *George Washington Carver National Monument*. 29 Oct. 2007 <http://www.nps.gov/archive/ gwca/expanded/quotes_2.htm>.

2. Linda McMurry. *George Washington Carver. Scientist and Symbol*. New York: Oxford University Press, 1981. 79.

3. "George Washington Carver." *BrainyQuote.com*. BrainyMedia.com. 2007. 13 July 2007 <http://www.brainyquote.com/quotes/quotes/ g/georgewash103591.html>.

4. The National Park Service. "Carver Quotes." *George Washington Carver National Monument*. 29 Oct. 2007 <http://www.nps. gov/archive/gwca/expanded/quotes_2.htm>.

Chapter 6. A Shining Star

1. American Chemical Society. "George Washington Carver: The Early Years." *ACS.org*. 2004. 29 Oct. 2007 <http://acswebcontent. acs.org/landmarks/landmarks/carver/earlyyears.html>.

2. The National Park Service. "Carver Quotes." *George Washington Carver National Monument*. 29 Oct. 2007 <http://www.nps.gov/archive/ gwca/expanded/quotes_2.htm>.

3. Gene Adair. *George Washington Carver*. New York: Chelsea House Publishers, 1989. 72.

4. U.S. Department of Agriculture. "About USDA." *USDA.com* 3 June 2004. 13 July 2007 <http://www.usda.gov/wps/portal/!ut/ p/_s.7_0_A/7_0_1OB/.cmd/ad/.ar/sa.retrievecontent/.c/6_2_ 1UH/.ce/7_2_5JN/.p/5_2_4TR/.d/0/_th/J_2_9D/_s.7_0_A/7_0_ 1OB?PC_7_2_5JN_navid=MISSION_STATEMENT&PC_7_2_5JN_ navtype=RT&PC_7_2_5JN_parentnav=ABOUT_USDA#7_2_5JN>.

SOURCE NOTES CONTINUED

Chapter 7. Bridging Troubled Waters
1. Georgia Humanities Council and the University of Georgia Press. "Commission on Interracial Cooperation." 2007. *GeorgeEncyclopedia.org*. 29 Oct. 2007 <http://www.georgiaencyclopedia.org/nge/Article.jsp?id=h-2919>.
2. YMCA.net. 29 Oct. 2007 <http://www.ymca.net/>.
3. USS *George Washington Carver* SSBN-656 Reunion Association. 2007. *gwcarver.org*. 29 Oct. 2007 <http://www.gwcarver.org/>.

Chapter 8. A Man of Great Faith
1. The National Park Service. "Carver Quotes." *George Washington Carver National Monument*. 29 Oct. 2007 <http://www.nps.gov/archive/gwca/expanded/quotes_2.htm>.
2. Gene Adair. *George Washington Carver*. New York: Chelsea House Publishers, 1989. 21.
3. Harvey Jay Hill. *He Heard God's Whisper*. Minneapolis, MN: Jorgenson Press, 1943. 14.
4. "George Washington Carver." *BetterWorld.net*. 13 July 2007 <http://www.betterworld.net/heroes/carver.htm>.
5. Linda McMurry. *George Washington Carver. Scientist and Symbol*. New York: Oxford University Press, 1981. 210.
6. Ibid. 208.
7. Tennessee Evolution Statutes, Chapter 27, Mar. 13, 1925. 13 July 2007 <http://www.law.umkc.edu/faculty/projects/ftrials/scopes/tennstat.htm>.
8. Gene Adair. *George Washington Carver*. New York: Chelsea House Publishers, 1989. 90.
9. The National Park Service. "Carver Quotes." *George Washington Carver National Monument*. 29 Oct. 2007 <http://www.nps.gov/archive/gwca/expanded/quotes_2.htm>.

Chapter 9. An Inspiration
1. Wastholm Media. 2006. *Aphorisms Galore!* 29 Oct. 2007 <http://www.ag.wastholm.net/aphorism/A-1225>.
2. Linda O. McMurry. *George Washington Carver: Scientist and Symbol.* New York: Oxford University Press, 1981. 260.
3. Ibid. 243–244.
4. Ibid. 240.
5. "The Field Museum Announces a New Traveling Exhibition: George Washington Carver." The Field Museum. 2007 14 July 2007 <http://www.fieldmuseum.org/exhibits/traveling_carver.htm>.

INDEX

ABOUT THE AUTHOR

Helga Schier was born in Germany and has a Ph.D. in language and literature. Schier has written and published works on a variety of subjects, including art, education, history, language, literature, and social studies. She lives in California with her husband and two children.

PHOTO CREDITS

AP Images, cover, 3, 6, 13, 49, 60, 75, 76, 85, 98 (bottom); Simon Smith/Getty Images, 8, 98 (top); AP/The Joplin Globe/ Vince Rosati, 14; Courtesy National Park Service, 20, 39, 41, 67, 96 (top); Iowa State University Library/Special Collections Department, 23, 27, 96 (bottom); Bettmann/Corbis, 28, 36, 42, 54, 68, 86, 89, 93, 97; Library of Congress/AP Images, 32, 50, 59; Corbis, 44; Sang Tan/AP Images, 81; The Joplin Globe/Vince Rosati/AP Images, 95, 99